Horse & pony CARE

1

The inspiration for this book lies in the depths of the Dorset countryside, where Danny resides.
Bryanston is one of the few places where the passing clip-clop of the horse is more common than the sound of the motor car.

Other titles by Danny :-

Danny Gets to Grips with **Gardening**
Danny Gets to Grips with **Golf**
Danny Gets to Grips with the **Motor Car**

Danny
GETS TO GRIPS WITH
Horse & pony CARE

First Published in1994

2nd Edition1995
by DC Publishing
11 Bryanston Village
Blandford Forum
Dorset DT11 0PR

Made and printed in Great Britain

This book is dedicated to the
girls in Danny's life......
his Mum, his Wife, his 3 daughters
and the cat.

CONTENTS

FOREWORD

"Look no further if you want to put the laughing into learning. There are some useful tips on Horse and Pony Care in this book, all moulded into some amusing cartoons.

Danny's sense of humour views some of the more mundane problems of horse-care with originality and inspiration.

_HAVE FUN__KICK ON__GIGGLE ON!_"

THE FIELD

The ideal field has shade-giving trees
and a stream providing fresh water.

The field should also have a water trough,
preferably with a mains supply.

Trees provide shelter from wind......

...... and sun.

The field should have good drainage,

and easy access.

The field should be harrowed from
time to time, to encourage new grass to grow.

It is essential that the field is checked &
cleared of any poisonous plants.

A simple shelter is a worthwhile
addition to the field.

It is important to remember to check the water,
especially during the Winter months.

Stagnant ponds must be
fenced off!

GATES & FENCES

It is essential that any field is securely fenced
and has a strong gate!

The fencing must be sufficiently high
to prevent the horse from jumping it.

Ponies are able to get through
very small gaps in fences.

A stone wall, provided that it is high enough,
makes a good fence.

Gate fastenings should be simple
for human beings to open......

......but impossible for the horse.

Barbed wire fences should
NEVER be used.

Fences should be checked
regularly for gaps.

Timber fences
are the safest.

THE STABLE

A stable needs water, electricity
and good drainage.

It needs to be weather-proof
& free from draughts!

The stable should be light & airy,
with plenty of room for the horse.

The floor must be non-absorbent,
hard-wearing & slip proof.

The stable ceiling must be high
enough for the horse to stand
comfortably.

Doors must be wide enough for
the horse to pass through easily.

Doors should be made in 2 halves
so that the top can be left open
for ventilation.

If a window is fitted, it should be placed
high enough on the wall opposite the
door & covered with an iron grille.

THE STABLE ROUTINE

A horse will be happy & settled in its
new home, if you develop a proper
routine.

Check the horse over
every day.

The routine should include regular
feeding times.

It's a good idea to work out
the stable routine

It should include time for
cleaning tack.

Looking after the horse takes less
time if the animal spends
part of the day in the field.

Livery can be arranged at a local stable
if you do not have the time to look after
your horse yourself.

If you are able to take good care of the
horse or pony yourself, I'm sure it will be
very rewarding .....
and of course, your animal will have
complete confidence in you!

THE STABLED HORSE

Stable care is best for the horse who is
going to be worked hard &
take part in shows.

A very well bred horse will not be able to
live out in all weathers.
He will certainly need to be stabled.

The stabled horse should be able to
see out, so that he can watch
the goings on in the yard.

It is important to work quietly
& calmly around the stabled horse.

When working with a stabled horse,
use your voice to tell him what you want
him to do.

Most horses that prove difficult
to handle in the stable have been made
that way by bad human handling.

FEEDING

1. Feed little and often......

2. ......Do not work the horse
immediately after a meal......

3. ......Provide plenty of water.

Feeding should be increased in
proportion to the demands of the
exercise routine.

The horse's diet should contain the
correct balance of proteins, fats,
starches & sugars, water, salts, fibre,
vitamins and minerals.

When possible, horses should be fed
at the same time everyday.

Fresh water should always be available.

The average horse will drink about
8 gallons of water per day.

Dusty or mouldy hay can cause
respiratory problems.

Feeding a horse properly is very
important. Always listen to advice or
seek assistance to achieve the
best diet.

SHOEING

Your horse's shoes should be checked
every day by yourself, and every 4-5 weeks
by your farrier.

Hoof oil, brushed on after cleaning,
will make the hooves look smart
and will also protect them from cracking.

GROOMING

The dandy brush is used to remove
surface dirt after the horse has been
worked or turned out.

A small sponge is useful for cleaning the
nostrils & wiping around the eyes.

Grooming is an important part of horse
care. It keeps the skin & coat healthy,
stimulates the circulation & because
most horses enjoy it, it can be a
pleasant time for both horse.....

...... and rider.

Particular care should be taken to keep
the horse's legs clean & mud free.

Clipping helps to keep the horse cool
when being worked hard & makes it
easier for grooming.

It is best, even in cold weather, not to
wear gloves when you are grooming.

Any tangles in the tail should be worked
loose with fingers before brushing.

Regular combing of the mane will keep
it in good condition & stop it getting
tangled or matted.

The horses hooves should be picked
out when grooming & also after
exercise.

An important part of the daily grooming
routine is a thorough overall
check of the horse.

BASIC HEALTH CARE

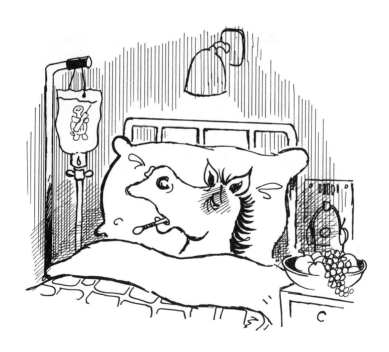

The healthy horse looks alert,
eyes bright......

......ears pricked......

......& carries his head high.

Equally important is the care of
your horse's teeth.

To keep him in good health, it is
important that the horse is not allowed
to get too hot......

......or too cold.

Most horses will benefit from having
their teeth rasped once a year.

To keep your horse free from worms,
he should be wormed at least
4 times each year.

A cut leg should be hosed down & the
wound carefully cleaned with
an antiseptic solution.

Although you can treat many minor
injuries yourself.......

.......never hesitate to call the vet
if you are not sure what to do.

MUCKING OUT
& BEDDING DOWN

Daily Mucking Out & Bedding
Down is an important part of
ensuring your horse's comfort.

Straw is a good bedding as it is warm
& comfortable for the horse to lie on.

Barley straw, however, may prove to be
an irritant......

......and oat straw is not recommended
as horses sometimes eat it.

Wood shavings are expensive but
easy to handle & are effective in
reducing dampness.

Paper provides a good bed, but loose
bits can cause a mess in the yard

Soiled bedding should be taken out
of the stable and added to
the manure heap..

EXERCISING

Daily exercise is essential
for all stabled horses.

Regular exercise prevents a horse
from becoming bored and listless.

A bored horse will develop
bad habits.

Lack of exercise can lead
to the horse becoming difficult to manage.

A controlled programme of steady,
regular work will produce
a horse with increased muscle.

An exercise programme should
finish in a walk, so that the horse returns
to his stable fairly cool & relaxed.